Published By Robert Corbin

@ Betty Tobias

The Complete Mediterranean Diet: Enjoy Quick & Simple Recipes to Build a Healthy Lifestyle

All Right RESERVED

ISBN 978-87-94477-04-8

TABLE OF CONTENTS

Fettuccine With Spinach And Shrimp 1

Style Salmon Burgers 3

Herbed Lamb And Roasted Veggies 7

Tuscan Tuna Salad 9

Breakfast Sandwich 11

Berry And Yogurt Parfait 13

Homemade Vegetable Pizza 14

Zucchini "Tagliatelle" 18

Slow-Cooked Buttery Mushrooms 20

Dairy-Free Pizza Crust: 21

Tuscan Beef Stew 23

Beef Stew 25

Spinach & Parsley Baked Omelet 27

English Breakfast 28

Pecan-Crusted Catfish 30

Sea Bass In A Pan With Peppers 32

Grilled Lemon Herb Mediterranean Chicken Salad 35

Avocado Toast 38

Homemade Vegetarian Mousse 40

Easy Zucchini Patties 43

Cheesy Spaghetti With Pine Nuts 45

Italian Chicken Pasta 47

Tuna And Couscous 49

Chickpeas, Spinach And Arugula Bowl 51

Coronate 53

Ravioli And Vegetable Soup 55

Oatmeal Banana Muffin 57

Almond And Maple Quick Grits 60

Spicy Escarole 62

Eggplant With Yogurt And Dill 63

Vegetarian Chili With Avocado Cream 65

Tomato And Avocado Salad 67

Chicken Salad With Grilled Pita 68

Halibut With Lemon-Fennel Salad 70

Italian Breakfast Frittata 72

Protein Oatcakes 74

Crusty Tuna Patties 76

Baked Teriyaki Salmon 78

Shrimp Salad For Two 81

Mediterranean Nachos 83

Parmesan Asparagus With Tomatoes 85

Cheesy Sweet Potato Burgers 87

Spaghetti With Anchovy Sauce 90

Parmesan Chicken 93

Tuna Pasta 95

Italian Minestrone Soup 98

Artichoke And Olive Salad 102

Sautéed Squash And Gorgonzola Polenta 103

Walnut And Date Breakfast Smoothie 105

Breakfast Quinoa Fruit Salad 106

Sautéed Collard Greens 108

Balsamic Bulgur Salad 110

Osseo Bunco 111

- Slow Cooker Beef Bourguignon 113
- Orange Ricotta Pancakes 117
- Scrambled Egg 119
- Lebanese Fatuous Salad 121
- Quinoa Granola 124
- Baked Vegetable Stew 127
- Freaked Pilaf With Dates And Pistachios 129
- Broccoli And Carrot Pasta Salad 132
- Chicken Quinoa Bowl 134
- Vegetable Risotto 137
- Tomato And Corn Soup 140
- Spinach Salad With Tuna 142
- Savoy Cabbage With Coconut Cream Sauce 144
- Sweet Potatoes Oven Fried 146
- Mango Salsa Chicken Burgers 148
- Roast Herb Turkey 150
- Artichoke Frittatas 152

Fettuccine With Spinach And Shrimp

Ingredients:

- 350 g medium raw shrimp, peeled, deveined
- 1/4 teaspoon crushed red pepper flakes
- 64 g crumbled feta cheese
- 1 teaspoon salt
- 1 package (280 g) frozen spinach, thawed
- 350 g whole-wheat fettuccine pasta, uncooked
- 3 garlic cloves, peeled, chopped
- 2 teaspoons dried basil, crushed
- 128 g sour cream

Directions:

1. In a large-sized mixing bowl, combine sour cream, the feta, basil, garlic, salt, and red pepper.
2. According to the package Directions:, cook the fettucine.
3. After the first 8 minutes of cooking, add the spinach and the shrimp to the boiling water with pasta; boil for 2 minutes more and then drain thoroughly.
4. Add the hot pasta, spinach, and shrimp mixture into the bowl with the sour cream mix; lightly toss and serve immediately.

Style Salmon Burgers

Ingredients:

- ½ tsp sweet paprika

- 1/2 tsp black pepper

- Kosher Salt

- Breadcrumbs for coating, about 40 g or so

- 30 g extra virgin olive oil

- 1 lemon

- 680 g skinless salmon fillet, cut into chunks

- 2 tsp Dijon mustard

- 2-3 tbsp minced green onions

- 120 g chopped fresh parsley

- 1 tsp ground coriander

- 1 tsp ground sumac

Salmon burger toppings

- Tzatziki Sauce or Maionaise

- 170 g baby arugula more to your liking

- 1 red onion, sliced

Directions:
1. Blend ¼ of the salmon together with the mustard until the mixture is pasty, then transfer to a bowl.
2. Blend the rest of the salmon so that it remains in pieces of about 0.5 cm; do not over blend it.
3. Once you have completed the process, put it in the same bowl as before.
4. Add the chopped green onions, parsley, spices (cilantro, sumac, paprika, black pepper) and salt to taste .

5. Stir everything together and then leave to chill in the refrigerator for about ½ hour.
6. While the salmon cools, prepare the toppings(wash the arugula, cut the tomatoes etc...).
7. Once the salmon has rested in the refrigerator, make 4 patties from the mixture.
8. Bread each patty in breadcrumbs and then arrange them on a baking sheet lined with baking paper.
9. Cook the patties in a frying pan with 3 tablespoons of oil for about 2-4 minutes.
10. Be careful that the oil should already be hot before you start to cook the patties.
11. The minimum internal temperature of the patties should be around 45-50 C to consider them cooked.
12. Once cooked, dry the excess oil well and season with additional salt and lemon juice if desired.

13. Now assemble the sandwiches by adding the tzatziki sauce (or mayonnaise) and garnish with the various toppings.

Herbed Lamb And Roasted Veggies

Ingredients:

- 1 tbsp. olive oil

- Pepper to taste

- 2 tbsp. mint leaves, chopped

- 1 tbsp. thyme leaf, chopped

- 8 lean lamb cutlets (fat removed)

- 1 onion, quarter cut

- 2 red bell peppers, chopped

- 2 zucchinis, sliced

- 1 sweet potato, peeled and chopped

Directions:

1. Preheat your oven to 425°F.

2. In a baking pan, put onion, pepper, zucchini and sweet potato.
3. Put inside the oven and roast for five minutes.
4. Drizzle with oil and sprinkle with black pepper.
5. Combine mint, thyme and pepper.
6. Use this to season the lamb cutlets.
7. Get the pan out of the oven and push vegetables to one side.
8. Put lamb cutlets in the middle and put back in the oven.
9. Roast until lamb is tender.

Tuscan Tuna Salad

Ingredients:

- 2 tbsp. lemon juice
- 2 tbsp. olive oil
- ¼ tsp. salt
- 15 oz. canned white beans
- 6 oz. canned light tuna flakes, drained
- 4 scallions, sliced
- 10 cherry tomatoes, quarter cut
- Pepper to taste

Directions:
1. Put tuna flakes, scallions, tomatoes, lemon juice, olive oil, salt and pepper in a bowl.
2. Toss to coat.

3. Chill in the refrigerator for a few minutes before serving.

Breakfast Sandwich

Ingredients:

- Pinch of kosher salt

- 4 eggs

- Ground black pepper to taste

- 2 cups of baby spinach leaves, fresh

- 1 tbsp. feta cheese

- 4 tsp. olive oil

- 1 tomato, sliced

- 4 multigrain sandwich thins

- 1 tbsp. Rosemary, fresh

Directions:

1. Set your oven to 375° Fahrenheit.

2. Place the sandwich thins on a baking sheet and drizzle 2 tsp of olive oil over the edges.
3. The edges should be lightly browned after about 5 minutes of baking time.
4. The remaining olive oil and rosemary are heated in a skillet over high heat.
5. Each egg should be cracked and added to the pan one at a time.
6. While the yolk should still be runny, the egg whites should be hard.
7. The yolks should be divided using a spatula.
8. Cook the egg until the other side is done.
9. Take the eggs away from the heat. Place the four sandwich thins on separate plates, then evenly spread the spinach among them.
10. Each thin is topped with two tomato slices, a cooked egg, and one tbsp of feta cheese.
11. Add a dash of salt and pepper to taste to season.

12. They are now prepared for serving; just add the remaining thin sandwich pieces on top.

Berry And Yogurt Parfait

Ingredients:

- 1/4 cup of chopped walnuts
- 1 1/2 cups of unsweetened nonfat plain Greek yogurt
- 1 cup of blackberries
- 1 cup of raspberries

Directions:
1. In two dishes or glasses, arrange the raspberries, yogurt, and blackberries. Put the walnuts on top, please.

Homemade Vegetable Pizza

Ingredients:

- 1 tbsp. Olive oil
- 3 cups white flour (you can also mix it with whole wheat or rye flour)
- Extra flour for
- Kneading cornmeal
- 1 cup water
- 2 tsp. Active dry
- Yeast pinch of sugar
- ½ tsp. Salt

Various toppings:

- Cheese (mozzarella, parmesan,
- Pecorino) red onions, thinly sliced
- Mushroom, sliced
- Bell pepper of different colors, sliced
- Broccoli florets,
- Torn artichoke
- Hearts, sliced olives,
- Pitted, sliced ripe
- Tomatoes, sliced
  walnuts, chopped

Directions:

1. Activate the yeast by setting it in water along with the sugar.

2. Permit it to represent 5 minutes or until the water starts to bubble. Then, add in the salt, oil, and a cup of flour.
3. Mix with a wooden spoon for quite some time to equally blend the flour in with the yeast.
4. To complete the batter, step by step add the excess flour a large portion of a cup at an at once after each clump. The subsequent batter ought to be delicate yet not sticky.
5. On a wooden surface, sprinkle flour and work the mixture for a very long time.
6. Permit the mixture to rest by setting in a bowl covered with oil. Cover it with plastic and put away for one hour until the batter rises.
7. Now, you are prepared to make the pizza. Split the mixture into four balls and utilizing the wooden surface, smooth each ball into the overall state of a pizza.

8. On a baking plate sprinkled with cornmeal, place two mixture circles each. Top every pizza with any blend of fixings that you like.
9. Preheat the stove to 500°F prior to placing in the pizza mixture. Permit it to prepare for around 12 minutes each. Serve hot.

Zucchini "Tagliatelle"

Ingredients:

- Chopped 2 tsp. Lemon peel , finely grated
- 4 tbsp. Fresh lemon juice
- 2 tbsp. Pistachio oil (or olive
- 1 large zucchini, peeled, seeded,
- Diced 1 cup white onion, finely chopped
- 1 ½ cups fresh mint leaves,
- Oil) salt and pepper

Directions:
1. Slice the zucchini into flimsy long strips. Try not profoundly.
2. To the zucchini, add the slashed onions, mint, and lemon strip.

3. Flavor by adding the lemon juice and pistachio or olive oil. Season with salt and pepper.
4. Serve cold by refrigerating as long as 3 hours before feast time.

Slow-Cooked Buttery Mushrooms

Ingredients:

- 3 cloves of garlic, minced
- 16 ounces fresh brown mushrooms, sliced
- 7 ounces fresh shiitake mushrooms, sliced
- A dash of thyme
- 2 tablespoons butter
- 2 tablespoons olive oil
- Salt and pepper to taste

Directions:
1. Heat the butter and oil in a pot.
2. Sauté the garlic until fragrant, around 1 minute.
3. Stir in the rest of the Ingredients: and cook until soft, around 9 minutes.

Dairy-Free Pizza Crust:

Ingredients:

- 6 large eggs

- 3 tablespoons psyllium husk powder

- Salt and black pepper, to taste

- 6 tablespoons Parmesan cheese

- 1(½) teaspoon Italian seasoning

Toppings:

- 4 ounces cheddar cheese

- 1 tablespoon mayonnaise

- 4 tablespoons tomato sauce

- 6 ounces rotisserie chicken, shredded

- 4 tablespoons BBQ sauce

Directions:

1. Warm the oven to 400ºF and grease a baking dish.
2. Place all the pizza crust Ingredients: in an immersion blender and blend until smooth.
3. Spread dough mixture onto the baking dish and transfer it to the oven. Bake for about 10 minutes and top with favorite toppings.
4. Bake for about 3 minutes and dish out.

Tuscan Beef Stew

Ingredients:

- 1 package McCormick Slow Cookers Hearty Beef Stew Seasoning
- ½ cup water
- ½ cup dry red wine
- 1 teaspoon rosemary leaves
- 8 slices Italian bread
- 2 pounds beef stew meat
- 4 carrots
- 2 (14 ½ ounce) cans tomatoes
- 1 medium onion

Directions:

1. Place the cubed beef in the slow cooker along with the carrots, diced tomatoes, and onion wedges.
2. Mix the seasoning package in ½ cup of water and stir well, making sure no lumps are remaining.
3. Pour the red wine over the water and stir slightly.
4. Add the rosemary leaves to the water-and-wine mixture, and then place the meat, stirring to ensure the meat is completely covered.
5. Switch the slow cooker to low, then cook for 8 hours, or 4 hours on high.
6. Serve with toasted Italian bread.

Beef Stew

Ingredients:

- ½ cup tomato sauce
- ¼ cup balsamic vinegar
- 1 can of black olives
- ½ cup garlic cloves
- 2 tablespoons fresh rosemary
- 2 tablespoons fresh parsley
- 1 tablespoon capers
- 1 tablespoon olive oil
- 8 ounces sliced mushrooms
- 1 onion
- 2 pounds chuck roast

- 1 cup beef stock

- 1 (14 ½ ounces) can tomatoes with juice

Directions:

1. Heat a skillet over high heat. Add 1 tablespoon of olive oil. Once heated, cook the cubed roast.
2. Once cooked, stir the rest of the olive oil (if needed), then toss in the onion and mushrooms.
3. When they have softened, transfer to the slow cooker.
4. Add the beef stock to the skillet to deglaze the pan, then pour it over the meat in the slow cooker.
5. Mix the rest of the Ingredients: to the slow cooker to coat.
6. Set the temperature on your slow cooker to low and cook for 8 hours.

Spinach & Parsley Baked Omelet

Ingredients:

- 1 tablespoon parsley, chopped

- ¼ cup spinach, chopped

- Salt and pepper to taste

- 1 teaspoon olive oil

- 3 eggs

- 3 tablespoons ricotta cheese

Directions:
1. Preheat your air fryer to 330°Fahrenheit. Whisk eggs adding salt and pepper as seasoning. Heat the olive oil in air fryer.
2. Stir in the ricotta, spinach, and parsley with eggs.

3. Pour the egg mixture into baking dish and cook in air fryer for 10-minutes. Serve warm.

English Breakfast

Ingredients:

- 1 can baked beans
- 2 tomatoes, sliced, sauté
- 1/2 cup mushrooms, finely sliced, sauté
- 1 tablespoon olive oil
- 8 medium sausages
- 8 slices of back bacon
- 4 eggs
- 8 slices of toast

Directions:

1. Preheat your air fryer to 320°Fahrenheit.

2. Heat olive oil in saucepan over medium-high heat. Add mushrooms to pan and sauté for a few minutes.
3. Then Remove mushrooms from pan and set aside, add tomatoes to pan and sauté for a few minutes then set aside.
4. Place your sausages and bacon into your air fryer and cook for 10-minutes.
5. Place the baked beans into a ramekin and your (cracked) eggs in another ramekin and cook for an additional 10-minutes at 390°Fahrenheit. Serve warm.

Pecan-Crusted Catfish

Ingredients:

- 1 cup pecans, chopped
- 2 Tbsp extra-virgin olive oil
- Salt & pepper, to taste
- 1 egg
- 2 Tbsp water
- 4 catfish fillets
- ½ cup flour

Directions:

1. Combine egg and water. Put fish in the mixture and let sit while preparing other ingredients.
2. Put flour on one sheet of wax paper, pecans on another.

3. Take each fish fillet from the egg mixture. Coat one side of fish in flour, other in pecans.
4. Cook fillets in the skillet for 5 minutes on each side.

Sea Bass In A Pan With Peppers

Ingredients:

- 3 Shallots, chopped

- Juice of ½ lemon

- ½ cup pitted Kalamata olives, chopped

- ½ tablespoon ground coriander

- ½ tablespoon garlic powder

- 1 teaspoon Aleppo pepper (or sweet spanish paprika)

- 1 teaspoon ground cumin

- 4 sea bass fillet, no skin

- 2 tablespoons olive oil (for cooking vegetables)

- ¼ cup olive oil (for cooking fish)

- Salt, to taste

- 1 Red Bell Pepper, cored and chopped

- 1 Green Bell Pepper, cored and chopped

- 4 garlic cloves, minced

- ½ teaspoon black pepper

Directions:

1. Sprinkle fish with salt on both sides and set aside.
2. Combine the spices in a small bowl to make the spice mixture.
3. Heat two tablespoons olive oil in a medium-sized skillet over medium-high heat. Add the bell peppers, shallots, and garlic. Season with salt and 1 teaspoon of the spice mixture. Cook, stirring, for 5 minutes.
4. Reduce the heat, and stir in the halved olives. Leave on low heat while preparing the fish.

5. Pat fish dry and season with the remaining spice mixture on both sides.
6. In a large skillet, heat ¼ cup olive oil over medium-high.
7. Add the fish pieces. Push down in the middle for 30 seconds or so. Cook fish on one side, until nicely browned, about 4-6 minutes.
8. Carefully turn fish over and cook on another side for 3-4 minutes until nicely browned.
9. Remove fish from heat, immediately drizzle with lemon juice.

Grilled Lemon Herb Mediterranean Chicken Salad

Ingredients:

Marinade/dressing:

- 1 teaspoon dried basil

- 1 teaspoons garlic, minced

- 0.5 teaspoon dried oregano

- 0.5 teaspoon salt

- Cracked pepper, to taste

- 0.5 pound (500 g) skinless, boneless chicken thigh fillets (or chicken breasts)

- 1 tablespoons olive oil

- Juice of 1 lemon (¼ cup fresh squeezed lemon juice)

- 1 tablespoon water

- 1 tablespoon red wine vinegar

- 1 tablespoon fresh chopped parsley

Salad:

- 0.5 red onion sliced

- 0.5 avocado sliced

- 0.17 cup pitted Kalamata olives (or black olives), sliced (optional)

- Lemon wedges to serve

- 2 cups Romaine (or Cos) lettuce leaves, washed and dried

- 0.5 large cucumber diced

- 1 Roma tomatoes diced

Directions:

1. Whisk together all of the marinade/dressing Ingredients: in a large jug.
2. Pour out half of the marinade into a large, shallow dish.
3. Refrigerate the remaining marinade to use as the dressing later.
4. Add the chicken to the marinade in the bowl; marinade chicken for 15-30 minutes (or up to two hours in the refrigerator if time allows).
5. While waiting for the chicken, prepare all of the salad Ingredients: and mix them in a large salad bowl.
6. Once the chicken is ready, heat one tablespoon of oil in a grill pan or a grill plate over medium-high heat.
7. Grill chicken on both sides until browned and cooked through.
8. Allow chicken to rest for 5 minutes; slice and arrange over salad.

9. Drizzle salad with the remaining UNTOUCHED dressing. Serve with lemon wedges.

Avocado Toast

Ingredients:

- 4 slices of toasted bread

- ½ cup feta cheese

- 1 cup cherry tomatoes halved

- ¼ cup basil

- 2 avocados

- 2 teaspoons lemon juice

- salt and pepper to taste

- Balsamic vinegar

Directions:

1. Cut the avocado in half and put the flesh in a small bowl.
2. Add lemon juice, salt, and pepper. With a fork, crush the Ingredients: together.
3. Spread the mixture over the toast.
4. Top with feta cheese, tomatoes, and basil.
5. Season to your liking with salt and pepper.
6. Pour a small trickle of balsamic vinaigrette on top.

Homemade Vegetarian Mousse

Ingredients:

- ½ tsp paprika

- ¼ cup parsley, chopped

- 1 tsp basil, chopped

- 1 tsp hot sauce

- 1 tomato, chopped

- 2 tbsp tomato puree

- 6 Kalamata olives, chopped

- ½ cup feta cheese, crumbled

- 2 tbsp olive oil

- 1 yellow onion, chopped

- 2 garlic cloves, chopped

- 2 eggplants, halved

- ½ cup vegetable broth

- Salt and black pepper to taste

Directions:

1. Preheat oven to 360 F. Remove the tender center part of the eggplants and chop it.
2. Arrange the eggplant halves on a baking tray and drizzle with some olive oil. Roast for 35-40 minutes.
3. Warm the remaining olive oil in a skillet over medium heat and add eggplant flesh, onion, and garlic and sauté for 5 minutes until tender.
4. Stir in the vegetable broth, salt, pepper, basil, hot sauce, paprika, tomato, and tomato puree.
5. Lower the heat and simmer for 10-15 minutes.

6. Once the eggplants are ready, remove them from the oven and fill them with the mixture.
7. Top with Kalamata olives and feta cheese. Return to the oven and bake for 10-15 minutes. Sprinkle with parsley.

Easy Zucchini Patties

Ingredients:

- 2 tablespoons chickpea flour
- 1 tablespoon chopped fresh mint
- 1 scallion, chopped
- 2 tablespoons extra-virgin olive oil
- 2 medium zucchinis, shredded
- 1 teaspoon salt, divided
- 2 eggs

Directions:

1. Put the shredded zucchini in a fine-mesh strainer and season with ½ teaspoon of salt. Set aside.

2. Beat together the eggs, chickpea flour, mint, scallion, and remaining ½ teaspoon of salt in a medium bowl.
3. Squeeze the zucchini to drain as much liquid as possible.
4. Add the zucchini to the egg mixture and stir until well incorporated.
5. Heat the olive oil in a large skillet over medium-high heat.
6. Drop the zucchini mixture by spoonful into the skillet. Gently flatten the zucchini with the back of a spatula.
7. Cook for 2 to 3 minutes or until golden brown. Flip and cook for an additional 2 minutes.
8. Remove from the heat and serve on a plate.

Cheesy Spaghetti With Pine Nuts

Ingredients:

- 4 tbsp. (½ stick) unsalted butter

- 1 tsp. freshly ground black pepper

- ½ cup pine nuts

- 8 oz. spaghetti

- 1 cup fresh grated Parmesan cheese, divided

Directions:

1. Bring a large pot of salted water to a boil. Add the pasta and cook for 8 minutes.
2. In a large saucepan over medium heat, combine the butter, black pepper, and pine nuts.
3. Cook for 2 to 3 minutes or until the pine nuts are lightly toasted.

4. Reserve ½ cup of the pasta water. Drain the pasta and put it into the pan with the pine nuts.
5. Add ¾ cup of Parmesan cheese and the reserved pasta water to the pasta and toss everything together to coat the pasta evenly.
6. To serve, put the pasta in a serving dish and top with the remaining ¼ cup of Parmesan cheese.

Italian Chicken Pasta

Ingredients:

- 1 cup mushrooms, diced
- 1/2 onion, diced
- 2 tomatoes, diced
- 2 cups of water
- 16 oz whole wheat penne pasta
- 1 lb chicken breast, skinless, boneless, and cut into chunks 1/2 cup cream cheese
- 1 cup mozzarella cheese, shredded
- 1 1/2 tsp Italian seasoning
- 1 tsp garlic, minced
- Pepper

- Salt

Directions:
1. Add all Ingredients: except cheeses into the inner pot of instant pot and stir well.
2. Seal pot with lid and cook on high for 9 minutes.
3. Once done, allow to release pressure naturally for 5 minutes then release remaining using quick release. Remove lid.
4. Add cheeses and stir well and serve.

Tuna And Couscous

Ingredients:

- 128 ml chicken stock
- 160 g of couscous
- A pinch of salt and black pepper
- 300 g canned tuna, drained and flaked
- 1 pint cherry tomatoes, halved
- 64 g pepperoncini, sliced
- 43 g parsley, chopped
- 1 tablespoon olive oil
- 32 g capers, drained
- Juice of ½ lemon

Directions:

1. Put stock in a pan, bring to a boil over medium-high heat, add the couscous and cook it.
2. Once cooked take it off the heat, cover, leave aside for 10 minutes, fluff with a fork and transfer to a bowl.
3. Add now tuna and the rest of the Ingredients:, toss and serve for lunch right away.

Chickpeas, Spinach And Arugula Bowl

Ingredients:

- 128 g of chickpeas, canned, drained
- ½ teaspoon of butter
- 250 g of tomatoes, chopped
- 1 cucumber, chopped
- 64 g of fresh spinach, chopped
- 64 g of arugula, chopped
- 64 g of lettuce chopped
- 1 tablespoon of olive oil
- 350 ml of chicken stock
- 4 teaspoons of hummus
- ½ teaspoon of salt

- ½ teaspoon of ground paprika

- ¾ teaspoon of onion powder

- 170 g of quinoa, dried

Directions:
1. Place the chickpeas in a skillet. Add the butter and salt.
2. Roast now chickpeas for 5 minutes over high heat. Stir from time to time.
3. Place quinoa and the chicken stock in the pan.
4. Cook quinoa for 15 minutes over medium heat.
5. Make the salad: combine cucumber, tomatoes, spinach, lettuce, arugula, olive oil. Shake salad gently.
6. Arrange now roasted chickpeas in every serving bowl.
7. Add now salad, hummus.
8. Add now quinoa.
9. Serve.

Coronate

Ingredients:

- 4 sticks celery, sliced
- ½ cup pine nuts, toasted
- ½ cup basil leaves, chopped
- 8 slices ciabatta
- 1 tbsp. olive oil
- 1 clove garlic, crushed
- ⅓ cup olive oil
- 3 eggplants, cubed
- 2 shallots, chopped
- 4 tomatoes, chopped
- 2 oz. raisins

- 2 tsp. unsalted capers

- 3 tbsp. red wine vinegar

Directions:
1. Warm olive oil in a pot over medium heat.
2. Cook eggplants for 20 minutes.
3. Remove eggplants from the pan.
4. Add shallots and cook for five minutes.
5. Add tomatoes and cook for 15 minutes.
6. Put back the eggplants and add raisins, capers, wine vinegar and celery.
7. Cover with the lid and simmer on low heat for 40 minutes.
8. While waiting, brush olive oil on the bread and rub garlic clove.
9. Grill the bread.
10. Garnish stew with nuts and basil.
11. Serve stew with the bread.

Ravioli And Vegetable Soup

Ingredients:

- ¼ tsp. red pepper, crushed

- 15 oz. canned vegetable stock

- 28 oz. canned crushed tomatoes

- 1½ cups hot water

- 1 tsp. dried basil

- 9 oz. frozen cheese whole-wheat ravioli

- 2 cups zucchini, diced

- 1 tbsp. olive oil

- 1 cup onion, diced

- 2 cloves garlic, minced

- 1 cup bell pepper, diced

- Pepper to taste

Directions:

1. Pour olive oil in a saucepan over medium heat.
2. Cook onion, garlic, red pepper and bell pepper for one to two minutes.
3. Add vegetable stock, tomatoes, water and basil.
4. Bring to a boil.
5. Add ravioli and cook according to package Directions:.
6. Add zucchini and cook for three minutes.
7. Sprinkle with pepper before serving.

Oatmeal Banana Muffin

Ingredients:

For the Muffins:

- 1 tbsp flax meal
- 1 banana, peeled
- 1 cup oats
- 1 tsp baking soda
- 1 tsp vanilla extract, unsweetened
- 1 tbsp honey
- 1/8 tsp salt
- 4 tbsp almond butter
- 1 tbsp yogurt
- 1 egg

For the Crumble:

- 1 tbsp honey

- 1 tbsp almond butter

- 4 ½ tbsp oats

- 1/8 tsp salt

Directions:
1. Turn on the oven, then lower the temperature to 350 degrees F and let it warm up.
2. In a medium bowl, mash one banana with a fork.
After adding these Ingredients:, whisk in the honey, egg, yogurt, and butter.
3. Oats, flax meal, baking soda, and salt should all be added. Stir until everything is combined.
4. Take six silicone muffin liners, place one inside each cup, and spoon the prepared batter into the liners in a uniform layer.

5. Place all of the Ingredients: for the crumb mixture in a small bowl, toss to combine, and then sprinkle over the muffin batter.
6. Bake the prepared muffins for 25 to 30 minutes, or until they are firm and the tops are golden brown.
7. Allow the muffins to cool fully before wrapping each piece in foil and plastic wrap.
8. Each muffin may be kept frozen for up to a month or in the fridge for up to five days.
9. When ready to eat, defrost a muffin in the refrigerator overnight, then reheat in the microwave for one minute.

Almond And Maple Quick Grits

Ingredients:

- 1/4 cup of pure maple syrup

- Pinch sea salt

- 1/4 cup of slivered almonds

- 1/2 tsp. ground cinnamon

- 1/2 cup of unsweetened almond milk

- 1/2 cup of quick-cooking grits

- 1 1/2 cups of water

Directions:

1. In a medium-sized saucepan, bring the water, almond milk, and sea salt to a boil over medium-high heat.
2. Add the grits gradually and mix continuously with a wooden spoon.

3. Bring the mixture to a low boil while stirring continuously to prevent lumps. Set the flame at a low intensity.
4. Stirring periodically, simmer for a few minutes or until all the water has been absorbed.
5. Stir the almonds and cinnamon into the syrup mixture while cooking for another minute.

Spicy Escarole

Ingredients:

- Pinch of red pepper
- Flakes 1 head of
- Escarole, torn salt and pepper
- 3 garlic cloves,
- Minced olive oil

Directions:

1. Sauté the garlic in olive oil for around 2 minutes.
2. Flavor with red pepper pieces prior to adding the escarole and afterward throwing in salt and pepper to taste.
3. Cover and cook for around 5 minutes. Serve warm.

Eggplant With Yogurt And Dill

Ingredients:

- ¼ cup olive oil
- ½ cup walnuts, toasted
- ½ cup plain yogurt
- ½ cup fresh
- 2 large eggplants,
- Chopped 3 shallots, chopped
- 3 garlic cloves, crushed
- Dill salt and pepper

Directions:

1. On a baking container fixed with a baking sheet, set out the cleaved eggplant along with the shallots and garlic.

2. Sprinkle with olive oil, salt and pepper to season.
3. Broil the elements for 30 minutes in a 400°F oven.
4. After 30 minutes, throw in the pecans, and add the yogurt, dill and more salt and pepper to season. Serve hot.

Vegetarian Chili With Avocado Cream

Ingredients:

- 1 1Red bell pepper, diced
- 1 Teaspoon ground cumin
- 1 1Tablespoons chili powder
- 1 Cups pecans, chopped
- 2 tablespoons olive oil
- 1/2 onion, finely chopped
- 1 Tablespoon minced garlic
- 1 Jalapeno peppers, chopped
- 1 Cups canned diced tomatoes and their juice

Topping:

- 1 avocado, diced

- 2 tablespoons fresh cilantro, chopped

- 1 cup sour cream

Directions:
1. Heat olive oil. Toss in the onion, garlic, jalapeno peppers, and red bell pepper, then sauté for about 4 minutes until tender.
2. Put in the chili powder and cumin and stir for 30 seconds.
3. Fold in the pecans, tomatoes, and their juice, then bring to a boil.
4. Simmer uncovered for about 20 minutes to infuse the flavors, stirring occasionally.
5. Remove from the heat to eight bowls.
6. Evenly top each bowl of chili with sour cream, diced avocado, and fresh cilantro.

Tomato And Avocado Salad

Ingredients:

- 1(½) tablespoon olive oil
- A handful of basil, chopped
- 1 pound cherry tomatoes, cubed
- 2 avocados, pitted, peeled, and cubed
- A pinch of sea salt and black pepper
- 2 tablespoons lemon juice
- 1 sweet onion, chopped

Directions:

1. In a salad bowl, mix the tomatoes with the avocados and the rest of the Ingredients:, toss and serve right away.

Chicken Salad With Grilled Pita

Ingredients:

- 1/4 cup lemon juice

- 3 tablespoons extra-virgin olive oil

- 1 tablespoon white wine vinegar

- 1/2 teaspoon chopped oregano

- 1/2 teaspoon salt, divided

- 1/4 teaspoon black pepper, divided

- 2 (6 inches) pitas

- 1/2 halved lengthwise and thinly sliced English cucumber

- 2 cups thinly sliced fennel bulb

- 1 cup shredded skinless, boneless rotisserie chicken breast

- 1/2 cup chopped flat-leaf parsley

- 1/4 cup vertically sliced red onion

Directions:
1. Preheat the oven to 350°F.
2. Situate pitas on a baking tray and bake for 12 minutes, cool down for 1 minute.
3. Cut into small pieces and combine with fennel, chicken, parsley, and red onion.
4. Season with ¼ teaspoon of salt and 1/8 teaspoon of pepper.
5. Add the juice, oregano, vinegar, the remaining ¼ teaspoon of salt, and 1/8 teaspoon of pepper.
6. Gradually add the oil, mixing with a whisk.
7. Season with dressing over the pita mixture to coat and serve.

Halibut With Lemon-Fennel Salad

Ingredients:

- 5 teaspoons extra-virgin olive oil, divided
- 1 teaspoon coriander
- 1/2 teaspoon salt
- ½ teaspoon cumin
- ¼ teaspoon ground black pepper
- 2 garlic cloves, minced
- 4 halibut fillets
- 2 cups thinly sliced fennel bulb
- ¼ cup thinly vertically sliced red onion
- 2 tablespoons lemon juice
- 1 tablespoon thyme leaves

- 1 tablespoon chopped flat-leaf parsley

Directions:

1. Combine the coriander, cumin, salt, and black pepper in a small bowl.
2. Combine 2 teaspoons of olive oil, garlic, and 1 ½ teaspoon of spice mixture in another small bowl, evenly rub the garlic mixture on the halibut.
3. Heat 1 teaspoon of oil in a large non-stick pan over medium-high heat.
4. Cook the halibut to the pan for 5 minutes.
5. Combine the remaining 2 teaspoons of oil, ¾ teaspoon of the spice mixture, the fennel bulb, onion, lemon juice, thyme leaves, and parsley in a bowl, mix well to coat, and serve salad with halibut. 427 39 20

Italian Breakfast Frittata

Ingredients:

- ½ teaspoon Italian seasoning

- 3 eggs

- 2-ounces parmesan cheese, shredded

- 1 tablespoon parsley, chopped

- 4 cherry tomatoes, sliced into halves

- ½ Italian sausage, sliced

- Salt and pepper to taste

Directions:

1. Preheat your air fryer to 360°Fahrenheit. Put the sausage and cherry tomatoes into baking dish and cook for 5-minutes.
2. Crack eggs into small bowl, add parsley, Italian seasoning and mix well by whisking.

3. Pour egg mixture over sausage and cherry tomatoes and place back into air fryer to cook for an additional 5-minutes. Serve warm.

Protein Oatcakes

Ingredients:

- 1/2 teaspoon cinnamon
- 60g curd
- 1 teaspoon cacao powder
- 15g sugar
- 70g oatmeal
- 15g protein
- 1 egg white
- 1/2 cup water

Directions:
1. Mix the oatmeal, protein, egg white, and water in a bowl.
2. Preheat a saucepan to medium heat.

3. Place the mixture into the saucepan.
4. While waiting, prepare the topping by mixing the curd, cinnamon, and sugar in a second bowl.
5. Remove the oatcake from the saucepan when it becomes golden-brown.
6. Serve on a plate.
7. Add the topping and cocoa powder.

Crusty Tuna Patties

Ingredients:

- 2 tablespoons chopped fresh parsley
- 2 tablespoons fresh chives, green onions or shallots, chopped
- Salt and pepper, to taste
- 1 egg
- A few dashes of Tabasco or Crystal hot sauce
- 2 tablespoons olive oil
- 2 (5 to 6-ounce) cans tuna, drained cans
- ½ cup white bread, torn into pieces
- 2 teaspoons Dijon mustard
- 1 tablespoon lemon juice

- 1 teaspoon lemon zest

- 1 tablespoon water or liquid from tuna

- ½ teaspoon butter

Directions:

1. In a medium bowl, mix the tuna, bread, mustard, lemon zest, water, lemon juice, parsley, hot sauce, chives, pepper, and salt.
2. Mix in the egg.
3. Divide the mixture into four parts. Form each part into a ball and make it into a patty.
4. Place on a wax paper-lined tray and chill for one hour.
5. Heat a little butter and the olive oil in a stick-free or a cast-iron skillet on medium-high.
6. Place the patties in the pan carefully, and cook until nicely golden-browned, 3-4 minutes on each side.

Baked Teriyaki Salmon

Ingredients:

- ¼ cup of soy sauce
- 1 cup of water
- 2 teaspoons minced garlic
- ¼ cup packed brown sugar
- ¼ teaspoon ground ginger
- 2 tablespoons honey
- 2 teaspoons sesame seeds
- ¼ cup of cold water
- 4 6-ounce salmon fillets
- ½ white or red onion, chopped
- 2 bell peppers, chopped

- 1 cup carrots, sliced

- 2 cups broccoli florets

- Salt and pepper, to taste

- 2 tablespoons oil

- 2 tablespoons corn starch

Directions:

1. Combine soy sauce, water, garlic, ginger, honey, and brown sugar in a medium saucepan and whisk together over medium-high heat. Bring to a boil.
2. Stir together corn starch and cold water until dissolved, then whisk into boiling sauce and lower heat to medium-low.
3. Remove from heat, stir in sesame seeds, and let the sauce cool.
4. Preheat the oven to 420° F.
5. Grease a baking sheet and place salmon fillets in the center.

6. In a large bowl, mix vegetables with oil, tossing to coat.
7. Put the vegetables around the salmon. Season everything with pepper and salt.
8. Drizzle ⅔ of the Teriyaki sauce over the veggies and salmon. Bake for 15-20 minutes, until veggies are easily pierced with a fork and salmon is flaky and tender.
9. Drizzle with remaining sauce and serve immediately.

Shrimp Salad For Two

Ingredients:

- ¼ teaspoon freshly ground pepper

- ½ teaspoon lemon juice

- 1 to 2 Tablespoons crumbled feta cheese

- ½ pound cooked shrimp

- ⅓ cup plain Greek yogurt

- ½ teaspoon dill mix

- 1 clove roasted garlic or use 1 teaspoon plain minced garlic if you like

- To serve: lettuce, olives, sourdough toast, pickled peppers, fresh parsley or dill and more feta cheese

Directions:

1. In a small bowl, stir together yogurt, spices, lemon juice, and cheese.
2. Set aside for 30 minutes at room temperature.
3. If using as a toast topper, chop the shrimp before tossing with the spiced yogurt.
4. If using shrimp in a salad, leave them whole and toss with the spiced yogurt or just plop a dollop of yogurt on top of the lettuce and pile the shrimp on top of that.
5. Serve over lettuce with olives, pickled peppers, and more feta, and be sure to toast up some sourdough to go alongside.
6. You can serve this salad in 2 ways--spread on toast or layered with preserved and fresh vegetables in a salad.

Mediterranean Nachos

Ingredients:

- 1 cup canned artichoke hearts, rinsed, drained, and squeezed dry of the liquid

- ½ cup chopped roasted red peppers patted dry from the jar

- ½ cup crumbled feta cheese

- 2½ Tablespoons pine nuts

- ½ cup chopped tomatoes

- ½ bag of tortilla chips

- ½ of a 10-ounce container of Sabra Hummus- any flavor

- ½ of 14.5 ounces can (~¾ cup) of garbanzo beans, rinsed, drained and patted dry

- 2 tablespoons fresh minced cilantro

Directions:

1. Preheat oven to 375 degrees. In an oven-safe cookie sheet or baking pan, layer tortilla chips, dollop with hummus, and spread slightly.
2. Top with garbanzo beans, artichoke hearts, red peppers, feta cheese, and pine nuts. Bake for ~5 minutes or until warm.
3. Remove from oven and top with fresh tomatoes and cilantro. Enjoy!

Parmesan Asparagus With Tomatoes

Ingredients:

- 10 Kalamata olives, chopped

- 2 lb asparagus, trimmed

- 2 tbsp fresh basil, chopped

- ¼ cup Parmesan cheese, grated

- Salt and black pepper to taste

- 3 tbsp olive oil

- 2 garlic cloves, minced

- 12 oz cherry tomatoes, halved

- 1 tsp dried oregano

Directions:

1. Warm 2 tbsp of olive oil in a skillet over medium heat sauté the garlic for 1-2 minutes,

stirring often, until golden. Add tomatoes, olives, and oregano and cook until tomatoes begin to break down, about 3 minutes; transfer to a bowl.
2. Coat the asparagus with the remaining olive oil and cook in a grill pan over medium heat for about 5 minutes, turning once until crisp-tender. Sprinkle with salt and pepper.
3. Transfer asparagus to a serving platter, top with tomato mixture, and sprinkle with basil and Parmesan cheese. Serve and enjoy!

Cheesy Sweet Potato Burgers

Ingredients:

- 1 garlic clove

- 1 cup old-fashioned rolled oats

- 1 tablespoon dried oregano

- 1 tablespoon balsamic vinegar

- ¼ teaspoon kosher salt

- 1 large sweet potato

- 2 tablespoons extra-virgin olive oil, divided

- 1 cup chopped onion

- 1 large egg

- ½ cup crumbled Gorgonzola cheese

Directions:

1. Using a fork, pierce the sweet potato all over and microwave on high for 4 to 5 minutes, until softened in the center.
2. Cool slightly before slicing in half.
3. Meanwhile, in a large skillet over medium-high heat, heat 1 tablespoon of the olive oil.
4. Add the onion and sauté for 5 minutes.
5. Spoon the sweet potato flesh out of the skin and put the flesh in a food processor.
6. Add the cooked onion, egg, garlic, oats, oregano, vinegar and salt. Pulse until smooth.
7. Add the cheese and pulse four times to barely combine.
8. Form the mixture into four burgers. Place the burgers on a plate, and press to flatten each to about ¾-inch thick.
9. Wipe out the skillet with a paper towel.
10. Heat the remaining 1 tablespoon of the oil over medium-high heat for about 2 minutes.

11. Add the burgers to the hot oil, then reduce the heat to medium.
12. Cook the burgers for 5 minutes per side.
13. Transfer the burgers to a plate and serve.

Spaghetti With Anchovy Sauce

Ingredients:

- 3 garlic cloves, minced
- 1/4 cup chopped fresh flat-leaf parsley
- 1 teaspoon red pepper flakes
- 1/4 teaspoon freshly ground black pepper
- Salt
- 1-pound spaghetti
- 1/4 cup extra-virgin olive oil
- 1 can oil-packed anchovy fillets, undrained
- 1 tablespoon bread crumbs

Directions:

1. Bring a large pot of water to a boil over high heat.
2. Once boiling, salt the water to your liking, stir, and return to a boil.
3. Add the spaghetti and cook according to package Directions: until al dente.
4. Drain, reserving about ½ cup of the cooking water.
5. Meanwhile, in a large skillet, heat the olive oil over low heat.
6. Add the anchovy fillets with their oil and the garlic.
7. Cook for 7 to 10 minutes, until the pasta, is ready, stirring until the anchovies melt away and form a sauce.
8. Add the spaghetti, parsley, red pepper flakes, black pepper, and a little of the reserved cooking water, as needed, and toss to combine all the Ingredients:.

9. Sprinkle with the bread crumbs.

Parmesan Chicken

Ingredients:

- 1 tsp. dried oregano

- ½ tsp. dried cilantro

- 1 tbsp. Panko bread crumbs

- One egg, beaten

- 1-pound chicken breast, skinless, boneless

- 2 oz. Parmesan, grated

- 1 tsp. turmeric

Directions:

1. Cut the chicken breast into three servings.
2. Then combine Parmesan, oregano, cilantro, bread crumbs, and turmeric.
3. Dip the chicken servings in the beaten egg carefully.

4. Then coat every chicken piece in the cheese-bread crumbs mixture.
5. Line the baking tray using the baking paper.
6. Arrange the chicken pieces in the tray.
7. Bake the chicken for 30 minutes at 365F.

Tuna Pasta

Ingredients:

- 2 cans (140 g each) solid albicore tuna, drained
- Zest of 1 lemon
- Juice of ½ lemon, more to your liking
- Handful chopped fresh parsley (about 1 ounce)
- 1 tsp dried oregano
- Black pepper, to your liking
- 6 to 8 pitted kalmata olives sliced
- 1 jalapeno pepper (optional), sliced
- 350 g spaghetti (or pasta of your choice)
- Kosher salt (I use Diamond Crystal)

- 180 g frozen peas

- Extra virgin olive oil (I use Private Reserve Greek extra virgin olive oil)

- 1 red bell pepper, cored and cut into thin strips

- 6 garlic cloves, minced

- Grated Parmesan cheese to your liking

Directions:
1. Boil 3 quarts of water and salt it.
2. Cook the pasta according to the Directions: on the package so that it is al dente.
3. After 5 minutes, add the frozen peas and cook them with the pasta for the rest of the time.
4. Before draining the pasta, take some of the cooking water and set it aside(about 120 g).
5. Take a frying pan and heat two tablespoons of oil in it.

6. Add the peppers and brown them for 3-4 minutes. The last 30 seconds, add the garlic.
7. Add the cooked pasta and peas to the pan and toss to combine.
8. Pour in the rest of the Ingredients: and stir everything together.
9. Add a little oil and use the cooking water to obtain a creamy consistency while stirring it.
10. Transfer the tuna pasta to serving bowls. Enjoy!

Italian Minestrone Soup

Ingredients:

- 1 can crushed tomatoes (400 g)
- 7 l of broth vegetable or chicken broth
- Parmesan cheese rind optional
- 1 bay leaf
- 2 to 3 springs fresh thyme
- 1 can kidney beans (400 g)
- Large handful chopped parsley
- Handful fresh basil leaves
- Grated parmesan cheese to serve (optional)
- 250 g already cooked small pasta such as ditalini or elbow pasta

- 30 g extra virgin olive oil see our olive oil options here

- 1 small yellow onion chopped

- 2 carrots chopped

- 2 celery stalks diced

- 4 garlic cloves minced

- 1 zucchini or yellow squash diced

- 120 g green beans fresh or frozen, trimmed and cut into 1-inch pieces, if needed

- Salt and pepper

- 1 tsp paprika

- 1/2 tsp rosemary

Directions:

1. In a large Dutch oven, add the oil and heat it over medium heat.

2. Once hot, put in the onions, carrots and celery and sauté, stirring regularly, for about 5 to 6 minutes.
3. Toward the end add the garlic and let it cook another minute.
4. Add the zucchini or yellow squash and green beans.
5. Season with paprika, rosemary, salt and pepper.
6. Stir to mix everything together.
7. Put the crushed tomatoes, broth, fresh thyme, bay leaf and parmesan rind (if you like) in the pot.
8. Bring to a boil then lower the heat so that the flame is low.
9. Partially cover the pot and let it cook for 20 minutes.
10. Add the green beans and cook for another 5-10 minutes.
11. Finally, add the parsley and fresh basil.

12. Put the pasta inside the soup and let it heat on low heat(it only needs to heat up not cook further).
13. Remove the cheese rind and bay leaf and serve.

Artichoke And Olive Salad

Ingredients:

- ⅓ cup low-fat mayonnaise
- ½ cup chopped olives
- ½ tsp. dried oregano
- 1 cup canned artichoke hearts, chopped
- 12 oz. canned chunk light tuna flakes, drained
- 2 tsp. lemon juice

Directions:
1. Put all Ingredients: in a bowl.
2. Toss to coat.

Sautéed Squash And Gorgonzola Polenta

Ingredients:

- 3 tbsp. garlic, minced

- 2 tbsp. olive oil

- 1 summer squash, cut into half lengthwise and sliced

- 2 zucchinis, cut into half lengthwise and sliced

- 2 tbsp. flour

- ¼ cup fresh basil, chopped

- 1 cup water

- 14 oz. canned vegetable stock, divided

- ½ tsp. pepper

- ¾ cup cornmeal

- ⅔ cup Gorgonzola cheese, crumbled

Directions:
1. Put water and half of the stock in a saucepan and boil.
2. Add pepper and cornmeal.
3. Stir until smooth. Reduce heat and cover.
4. Keep cooking while stirring occasionally.
5. Wait for consistency to become thick.
6. Add gorgonzola.
7. Remove it from heat.
8. In a skillet, heat oil and cook garlic for one minute.
9. Cook squash and zucchini for five minutes.
10. Dust flour on top of the vegetables.
11. Mix to coat.
12. Add remaining stock. Bring to a boil.
13. Simmer and cook for three more minutes.
14. Put the sautéed vegetables on top of the polenta.
15. Sprinkle basil on top before serving.

Walnut And Date Breakfast Smoothie

Ingredients:

- 2 cups of plain Greek yogurt
- 2 to 3 ice cubes
- 1/2 cup of walnuts
- 1/2 tsp pure vanilla extract
- 1/2 cup of milk
- 1/2 tsp. ground cinnamon
- 4 dates, pitted

Directions:

1. All the components should be blended in a blender until smooth. Offer cold.

Breakfast Quinoa Fruit Salad

Ingredients:

- 2 tbsp. lime juice
- 2 kiwis, peeled and quartered
- 1 tsp. chopped fresh basil
- 1 mango, peeled, pitted and diced
- 1 cup of cooked quinoa
- 2 tbsp. raw honey
- 1 peach, pitted and diced
- 1 cup of strawberries, fresh and sliced
- 1 cup of blackberries

Directions:

1. In a small mixing bowl, blend the lime juice, basil, and honey.

2. In another dish, mix the strawberries, quinoa, kiwis, blackberries, peaches, and mango.
3. Pour the honey mixture over the fruit and toss to coat before serving.

Sautéed Collard Greens

Ingredients:

- 1 teaspoon pepper
- 1 teaspoon salt
- 2 cloves garlic, minced
- 1 large onion, chopped
- 3 slices bacon
- 1 pound fresh collard greens, cut into 2-inch pieces
- 1 pinch red pepper flakes
- 3 cups chicken broth
- 1 tablespoon olive oil

Directions:

1. Using a large skillet, heat oil on medium-high heat.
2. Sauté bacon until crisp. Remove it from the pan and crumble it once cooled. Set it aside.
3. Using the same pan, sauté onion and cook until tender.
4. Add garlic until fragrant. Add the collard greens and cook until they start to wilt.
5. Pour in the chicken broth and season with pepper, salt, and red pepper flakes.
6. Reduce the heat to low and simmer for 45 minutes.

Balsamic Bulgur Salad

Ingredients:

- A pinch of sea salt and black pepper
- 2 tablespoons lemon juice
- 2 tablespoons balsamic vinegar
- ¼ cup olive oil
- 1 cup bulgur
- 2 cups hot water
- 1 cucumber, sliced

Directions:

1. In a bowl, mix bulgur with the water, cover, leave aside for 30 minutes, fluff with a fork, and transfer to a salad bowl.
2. Add the rest of the Ingredients:, toss and serve.

Osseo Bunco

Ingredients:

- 2 celery stalks, diced
- 4 garlic cloves, minced
- 1 (14 ounces) can diced tomatoes
- 2 teaspoons dried thyme leaves
- ½ cup beef or vegetable stock
- 4 beef shanks or veal shanks
- 1 teaspoon sea salt
- ½ teaspoon ground black pepper
- 3 tablespoons whole wheat flour
- 1-2 tablespoons olive oil
- 2 medium onions, diced

- 2 medium carrots, diced

Directions:

1. Season the shanks on both sides, then dip in the flour to coat.
2. Warm a large skillet over high heat. Add the olive oil.
3. Once hot, situate the shanks and brown evenly on both sides.
4. When browned, transfer to the slow cooker.
5. Pour the stock into the skillet and let simmer for 3-5 minutes while stirring to deglaze the pan.
6. Incorporate the rest of the Ingredients: into the slow cooker and pour the stock from the skillet over the top.
7. Click slow cooker to low and cook for 8 hours.
8. Serve the Osso Bucco over quinoa, brown rice, or even cauliflower rice.

Slow Cooker Beef Bourguignon

Ingredients:

- ½ teaspoon pepper
- 2 tablespoons whole-wheat flour
- 12 small pearl onions
- 3 cups red wine
- 2 cups beef stock
- 2 tablespoons tomato paste
- 1 beef bouillon cube
- 1 teaspoon fresh thyme
- 2 tablespoons fresh parsley
- 2 bay leaves
- 2 tablespoons butter

- 1 tablespoon extra-virgin olive oil

- 6 ounces bacon

- 3 pounds beef brisket

- 1 large carrot

- 1 large white onion

- 6 garlic cloves

- ½ teaspoon coarse salt

- 1 pound mushrooms

Directions:
1. Preheat the skillet over medium-high heat, pour the olive oil.
2. When it has heated, cook the bacon until it is crisp, then place it in your slow cooker. Save the bacon fat in the skillet.

3. Pat-dry the beef with a paper towel and cook it in the same skillet with the bacon fat until all sides have the same brown coloring.
4. Transfer to the slow cooker.
5. Add the onion and carrot to the slow cooker and season with salt and pepper.
6. Stir to combine the Ingredients: and make sure everything is seasoned.
7. Pour the red wine into the skillet and simmer for 4-5 minutes to deglaze the pan, then stir in the flour, stirring until smooth.
8. When the liquid has thickened, pour it into the slow cooker and stir to coat everything with the wine mixture.
9. Add the tomato paste, bouillon cube, thyme, parsley, 4 cloves of garlic, and bay leaves.
10. Adjust your slow cooker to high and cook for 6 hours or 8 hours on low.
11. Before serving, heat the butter in a skillet over medium heat.

12. When the oil is hot, add the remaining 2 cloves of garlic and cook for about 1 minute before adding the mushrooms.
13. Cook the mushrooms until soft, then add to the slow cooker and mix to combine.
14. Serve with mashed potatoes, rice, or noodles.

Orange Ricotta Pancakes

Ingredients:

- 3 separated eggs
- 1 cup fresh ricotta
- 3/4 cup whole milk
- 1/2 teaspoon pure vanilla extract
- 1 large ripe orange
- 3/4 cup all-purpose flour
- 1/2 tablespoon baking powder
- 2 teaspoons sugar
- 1/2 teaspoon salt

Directions:

1. Using bowl Mix the flour, baking powder, sugar in a large bowl.

2. Add a pinch of salt.
3. In a separate bowl, whisk egg yolk, ricotta, milk, orange zest, and orange juice.
4. Add some vanilla extract for additional flavor.
5. Followed by the dry Ingredients: to the ricotta mixture and mix adequately.
6. Stir the egg white in a different bowl, and then gently fold it in the ricotta mixture.
7. Preheat saucepan to medium heat and brush with some butter until evenly spread.
8. Use a measuring cup to drop the batter onto the saucepan, ensure the pan is not crowded.
9. Allow cooking for 2 minutes.
10. Flip the food when you notice the edges begin to set, and bubbles form in the center.
11. Cook the meat for another 1 to 2 minutes.
12. Serve with any toppings of your choice.

Scrambled Egg

Ingredients:

- 1/8 teaspoon white pepper
- 1 tablespoon Olive oil
- 1 large egg
- 1/2 teaspoons light soy sauce

Directions:

1. Beat the eggs in a bowl.
2. To the beaten egg, add soy sauce, one-teaspoon Olive oil, and pepper.
3. Preheat a saucepan on high heat.
4. Add the two tablespoons oil to the saucepan.
5. Then add the mixture of the beaten egg.
6. The edges will begin to cook.
7. Lessen the heat to medium and carefully scramble the eggs.

8. After that Turn off heat and transfer into a bowl.
9. Serve hot and enjoy

Lebanese Fatuous Salad

Ingredients:

Salad

- 0.5 large vine-ripe tomato diced
- 1-1.5 Persian cucumbers quartered
- 0.25 a large green pepper chopped
- 2.5 radishes diced
- 1 green onions/scallions chopped
- 0.13 cup fresh chopped parsley
- 0.5 large double ply pita bread cut into triangles
- 1.5 tablespoon olive oil
- Kosher salt to taste
- Freshly cracked pepper to taste

- 0.5 large head of romaine lettuce chopped

Dressing

- 0.5 teaspoon pomegranate molasses substitute balsamic glaze

- 0.25 teaspoon mint fresh or dried

- 0.25 teaspoon kosher salt

- Fresh cracked black pepper to taste

- 1.5 tablespoon olive oil

- 1 tablespoon lemon juice

- 1 garlic clove pressed or grated

- 0.5 teaspoon sumac substitute grated lemon zest

Directions:

1. In a large skillet, heat three tablespoons of extra virgin olive oil on medium heat.

2. Add the pita bread and season with kosher salt and freshly cracker peppers.
3. Fry the pita for 5-7 minutes until the pieces are crispy and golden in color. (Alternatively, bake the pita bread at 425F° for 5-10 minutes.) Set the fried bread aside.
4. In a large bowl, add the salad dressing Ingredients: olive oil, lemon juice, garlic, sumac, pomegranate molasses, mint, salt, and pepper.
5. Whisk together until the dressing is emulsified and well blended.
6. Add the lettuce, tomatoes, cucumbers, green peppers, radishes, green onions, and parsley to the large bowl of dressing and toss to combine.
7. Add the fried pita bread to the salad immediately before serving and gently toss again.
8. Serve chilled or at room temperature.

Quinoa Granola

Ingredients:

- 1 Tbsp coconut sugar (or sub organic brown sugar, muscovado, or organic cane sugar)
- 1 pinch sea salt
- 3 ½ Tbsp coconut oil
- ¼ cup maple syrup (or agave nectar)
- 1 cup Rolled Oats (gluten-free for GF eaters)
- ½ cup uncooked White Quinoa
- 2 cups raw almonds (roughly chopped)

Directions:
1. Pre heat oven to 340 degrees F (171 C).
2. Add oats, quinoa, almonds, coconut sugar, and salt to a large mixing bowl - stir to combine.

3. To a small saucepan, add coconut oil and maple syrup.
4. Warm over medium heat for 2-3 minutes, whisking frequently until the two are combined and there is no visible separation.
5. Immediately pour over the dry Ingredients: and stir to combine until all oats and nuts are thoroughly coated.
6. Arrange on a large baking sheet and spread into an even layer.
7. Bake for 20 minutes. Then remove from oven and stir/toss the granola.
8. Turn the pan around so the other end goes into the oven first (so it bakes evenly) and bake 5-10 minutes more.
9. Watch carefully as to not burn. You'll know it's done when the granola is deep golden brown and very fragrant.
10. Let cool completely before enjoying.

11. Store leftovers in a sealed bag or container at room temperature for 2 weeks or in the freezer for up to 1 month.

Baked Vegetable Stew

Ingredients:

- 1 ½ lb green beans, sliced
- 1 lb Yukon Gold potatoes, peeled and chopped
- 1 tbsp tomato paste
- Salt and black pepper to taste
- 3 tbsp fresh basil, chopped
- 1 can diced tomatoes, drained with juice reserved
- 3 tbsp olive oil
- 1 onion, chopped
- 2 tbsp fresh oregano, minced
- 1 tsp paprika

- 4 garlic cloves, minced

Directions:

1. Preheat oven to 360 F. Warm the olive oil in a skillet over medium heat.
2. Sauté onion and garlic for 3 minutes until softened.
3. Stir in oregano and paprika for 30 seconds.
4. Transfer to a baking dish and add in green beans, potatoes, tomatoes, tomato paste, salt, pepper, and 1 ½ cups of water; stir well.
5. Bake for 40-50 minutes. Sprinkle with basil. Serve.

Freaked Pilaf With Dates And Pistachios

Ingredients:

- Salt and pepper, to taste

- 1¾ cups water

- 1½ cups cracked freekeh, rinsed

- 3 ounces pitted dates, chopped

- ¼ cup shelled pistachios, toasted and coarsely chopped

- 1½ tablespoons lemon juice

- ¼ cup chopped fresh mint

- 2 tablespoons extra-virgin olive oil, plus extra for drizzling

- 1 shallot, minced

- 1½ teaspoons grated fresh ginger

- ¼ teaspoon ground coriander

- ¼ teaspoon ground cumin

Directions:

1. Set the Instant Pot to Sauté mode and heat the olive oil until shimmering.
2. Add the shallot, ginger, coriander, cumin, salt, and pepper to the pot and cook for about 2 minutes, or until the shallot is softened.
3. Stir in the water and freekeh.
4. Secure the lid. Select the Manual mode and set the cooking time for 4 minutes at High Pressure.
5. Once cooking is complete, do a quick pressure release. Carefully open the lid.
6. Add the dates, pistachios and lemon juice and gently fluff the freekeh with a fork to combine. Season to taste with salt and pepper.

7. Transfer to a serving dish and sprinkle with the mint. Serve drizzled with extra olive oil.

Broccoli And Carrot Pasta Salad

Ingredients:

- ¼ cup plain Greek yogurt

- Juice of 1 lemon

- 1 teaspoon red pepper flakes

- 8 ounces (227 g) whole-wheat pasta

- 2 cups broccoli florets

- 1 cup peeled and shredded carrots

- Sea salt and freshly ground pepper, to taste

Directions:
1. Bring a large pot of lightly salted water to a boil.
2. Add the pasta to the boiling water and cook until al dente.
3. Drain and let rest for a few minutes.

4. When cooled, combine the pasta with the veggies, yogurt, lemon juice, and red pepper flakes in a large bowl, and stir thoroughly to combine.
5. Taste and season to taste with salt and pepper. Serve immediately.

Chicken Quinoa Bowl

Ingredients:

- 16 g feta cheese, crumbled

- ½ teaspoon salt

- 1 small garlic clove, crushed

- 230 g boneless, skinless chicken breasts, trimmed

- ½ (200 g) jar roasted red peppers, rinsed

- ½ teaspoon paprika

- 16 g pitted Kalamata olives, chopped

- 64 g cucumber, diced

- ¼ teaspoon ground cumin

- 64 g almonds, slivered

- 1/8 teaspoon black pepper

- 2 tablespoons extra-virgin olive oil, divided

- 1/8 teaspoon crushed red pepper

- 1 tablespoon fresh parsley, finely chopped

- 128 g cooked quinoa

- 16 g red onions, finely chopped

Directions:

1. Preheat the oven on broiler setting and lightly grease a baking sheet.
2. Sprinkle the chicken with salt and black pepper.
3. Transfer it on the baking sheet and broil for about 15 min.
4. Let the chicken cool for about 5 min and transfer to a cutting board.
5. Shred the chicken and keep aside.

6. Put almonds, paprika, black pepper, garlic, half of olive oil, red pepper and cumin in a blender.
7. Blend until smooth and dish out in a bowl.
8. Toss quinoa, red onions, 2 tablespoons oil, quinoa and olives in a bowl.
9. Divide the quinoa mixture in the serving bowls and top with cucumber, red pepper sauce and chicken.
10. Garnish with feta cheese and parsley to immediately serve.

Vegetable Risotto

Ingredients:

- 100 ml dry vermouth or white wine (optional)

- 2 pinches dried flaked chilies (crushed chillies)

- Lemon zest from 1 lemon, finely grated

- 2 garlic cloves, finely chopped

- 50 g grated Parmesan, plus extra to serve

- Salt and freshly ground black pepper (optional)

- Freshly chopped parsley, to serve (optional)

- 1 L stock broth (made with 1 vegetable or chicken stock cube)

- 1 large onion, chopped

- 2 medium carrots, cut into 1cm chunks

- 2 celery sticks, trimmed and cut into roughly 1cm chunks

- 3 tbsp olive oil

- 275 g rice for risotto, such as Arborio

Directions:

1. Heat the oil in a large saucepan or medium flameproof casserole.
2. Sauté the onion, carrots, and celery for 10 to 12 minutes, taking care to stir so they do not stick to the bottom of the pan.
3. Toward the end add the garlic and cook for another 2 minutes.
4. Add the rice and toast it for 1 minute, stirring constantly (it should not stick).
5. Deglaze with vermouth (or wine, if using) and evaporate the alcohol by cooking for 30-40 seconds.
6. Pour the stock and chili into the pot. Bring to a boil over medium heat and cook without a

lid for 22-25 minutes, or until the rice is tender and very creamy.
7. Stir the risotto every 4 to 5 minutes for the first 10 minutes of cooking, then more regularly as the liquid reduces and the rice swells; stir constantly for the last 5 minutes.
8. Once cooked, add the lemon zest and cheese.
9. Season with salt and pepper and serve with more Parmesan cheese and chopped fresh parsley, if desired.

Tomato And Corn Soup

Ingredients:

- 1 tsp. olive oil

- Salt and pepper to taste

- ¼ tsp. Worcestershire sauce

- 1 tsp. tomato paste

- 2 cups low-sodium chicken stock, divided

- 1 tbsp. basil, chopped

- ½ cup corn kernels

- 1 sweet onion, sliced

- 1½ lb. tomatoes, sliced

- 3 cloves garlic, unpeeled

- 1 tbsp. olive oil

Directions:

1. Preheat your oven to 400°F.
2. Coat your baking pan with cooking spray.
3. In a bowl, pour one tablespoon olive oil.
4. Add onion, garlic and tomatoes. Sprinkle salt and pepper.
5. Toss to coat. Put these on the baking pan and roast for 30 minutes.
6. Remove the seeds from the tomatoes and the ends in the onion.
7. Peel the cloves of garlic.
8. Blend these in a food processor with one cup stock and remaining oil.
9. Pour mixture in a pot.
10. Add remaining stock, tomato paste, tomato juice, basil, brown sugar and Worcestershire sauce.
11. Simmer for a few minutes.
12. Garnish with corn before serving.

Spinach Salad With Tuna

Ingredients:

- 5 oz. canned chunk light tuna flakes in water, drained
- 2 cups baby spinach
- 2 tbsp. parsley
- 2 tbsp. feta cheese
- 1½ tbsp. freshly-squeezed lemon juice
- 1½ tbsp. water
- 1½ tbsp. tahini
- 4 pieces Kalamata olives, pitted and chopped

Directions:

1. Combine lemon juice, water and tahini in a bowl.

2. Add olives, tuna, feta, and parsley.
3. Pour mixture on top of spinach before serving.

Savoy Cabbage With Coconut Cream Sauce

Ingredients:

- 2 cups bone broth
- 1 cup coconut milk, freshly squeezed
- 1 bay leaf
- Salt and pepper to taste
- 2 tablespoons chopped parsley
- 3 tablespoons olive oil
- 1 onion, chopped
- 4 cloves of garlic, minced
- 1 head savoy cabbage, chopped finely

Directions:

1. Heat oil in a pot for 2 minutes.

2. Stir in the onions, bay leaf, and garlic until fragrant, around 3 minutes.
3. Add the rest of the Ingredients:, except for the parsley, and mix well.
4. Cover pot, bring to a boil, and let it simmer for 5 minutes or until cabbage is tender to taste.
5. Stir in parsley and serve.

Sweet Potatoes Oven Fried

Ingredients:

- 1 tablespoon fresh parsley, chopped finely

- ¼ teaspoon pepper

- ¼ teaspoon salt

- 1 tablespoon olive oil

- 1 small garlic clove, minced

- 1 teaspoon grated orange rind

- 4 medium sweet potatoes, peeled and sliced into a ¼-inch thickness

Directions:

1. In a large bowl mix well pepper, salt, olive oil, and sweet potatoes.
2. In a greased baking sheet, in a single layer arrange sweet potatoes.

3. Pop in a preheated 400ºF oven and bake for 15 minutes, turnover potato slices, and return to oven.
4. Bake for another 15 minutes or until tender.
5. Meanwhile, mix well in a small bowl, garlic, orange rind, and parsley, sprinkle over cooked potato slices, and serve.
6. You can store baked sweet potatoes in a lidded container and just microwave whenever you want to eat them.
7. Consume within 3 days.

Mango Salsa Chicken Burgers

Ingredients:

- 2 mangos, peeled, pitted, and cubed

- ½ red onion, finely chopped

- 1 lime juice

- 1 garlic clove, minced

- ½ jalapeno pepper, seeded and finely minced

- 2 tablespoons chopped fresh cilantro leaves

- 1 ½ pound ground turkey breast

- 1 teaspoon sea salt, divided

- ¼ teaspoon freshly ground black pepper

- 2 tablespoons extra-virgin olive oil

Directions:

1. Form the turkey breast into 4 patties and season with ½ teaspoon of sea salt and pepper.
2. Cook the olive oil in a non-stick skillet until it shimmers.
3. Cook for about 5 minutes per side until the turkey patties are browned. In a separate bowl, combine the mangos, red onion, lime juice, garlic, jalapeno, cilantro, and the remaining 1/2 teaspoon of sea salt while the patties are cooking.
4. Serve the salsa on top of the turkey patties.

Roast Herb Turkey

Ingredients:

- 2 tablespoons chopped fresh Italian parsley leaves
- 1 teaspoon ground mustard
- 1 teaspoon sea salt
- ¼ teaspoon freshly ground black pepper
- 1 (6 pounds) bone-in, skin-on turkey breast
- 2 tablespoons extra-virgin olive oil
- 4 garlic cloves, minced
- 1 lemon zest
- 1 tablespoon chopped fresh thyme leaves
- 1 tablespoon chopped fresh rosemary leaves

- 1 cup dry white wine

Directions:

1. Preheat the oven to 325°F.
2. Combine the olive oil, garlic, lemon zest, thyme, rosemary, parsley, mustard, sea salt, and pepper.
3. Brush the herb mixture evenly over the surface of the turkey breast, loosen the skin and rub underneath as well.
4. Situate the turkey breast in a roasting pan on a rack, skin-side up.
5. Pour the wine into the pan. Roast for 1 or 1 hour and 30 minutes until the turkey reaches an internal temperature of 165ºF.
6. Pull out from the oven and set separately for 20 minutes, tented with aluminum foil to keep it warm, before carving.

Artichoke Frittatas

Ingredients:

- Green onions
- Dried tomatoes
- Two eggs
- Italian seasoning
- oz. dry spinach
- 1/4 red bell pepper
- Artichoke (drain the liquid)
- Salt - Pepper

Directions:
1. Preheat oven to medium heat.
2. Brush a bit of oil on the cast-iron skillet.
3. Mix all the vegetables.

4. Add some seasoning.
5. Spread the vegetables evenly in the pan.
6. Whisk the eggs and add some milk.
7. Add some salt and pepper.
8. Mix in some cheese (helps to make it fluffier).
9. Pour the egg mixture in the saucepan.
10. Place the pan inside the oven for about 30 minutes.
11. Enjoy!

www.ingramcontent.com/pod-product-compliance
Lightning Source LLC
LaVergne TN
LVHW010217070526
838199LV00062B/4627